THINKER'S GUIDE LIBRARY

思想者指南系列丛书

PRACTICAL WAYS FOR PROMOTING ACTIVE AND COOPERATIVE LEARNING

如何促进主动学习与合作学习

(美) Wesley Hiler (美) Richard Paul 著

外语教学与研究出版社
FOREIGN LANGUAGE TEACHING AND RESEARCH PRESS
北京 BEIJING

京权图字：01-2016-3337

图书在版编目（CIP）数据

如何促进主动学习与合作学习 ：英文 ／（美）希勒（Hiler, W.），（美）保罗（Paul, R.）著. —— 北京 ：外语教学与研究出版社，2016.4（2016.6重印）
（思想者指南系列丛书）
ISBN 978-7-5135-7472-3

Ⅰ. ①如… Ⅱ. ①希… ②保… Ⅲ. ①大学生－学习方法－英文 Ⅳ. ①G642.46

中国版本图书馆CIP数据核字（2016）第097154号

出 版 人　蔡剑峰
项目负责　任　佼
责任编辑　任　佼
封面设计　孙莉明
出版发行　外语教学与研究出版社
社　　址　北京市西三环北路19号（100089）
网　　址　http://www.fltrp.com
印　　刷　北京联兴盛业印刷股份有限公司
开　　本　850×1168　1/32
印　　张　1
版　　次　2016年5月第1版 2016年6月第2次印刷
书　　号　ISBN 978-7-5135-7472-3
定　　价　7.90 元

购书咨询：（010）88819926　电子邮箱：club@fltrp.com
外研书店：https://waiyants.tmall.com
凡印刷、装订质量问题，请联系我社印制部
联系电话：（010）61207896　电子邮箱：zhijian@fltrp.com
凡侵权、盗版书籍线索，请联系我社法律事务部
举报电话：（010）88817519　电子邮箱：banquan@fltrp.com
法律顾问：立方律师事务所　刘旭东律师
　　　　　中咨律师事务所　殷　斌律师
物料号：274720001

序　言

思辨能力或者批判性思维由两个维度组成，在情感态度层面包括勤学好问、相信理性、尊重事实、谨慎判断、公正评价、敏于探究、持之以恒地追求真理等一系列思维品质或心理倾向；在认知层面包括对证据、概念、方法、标准、背景等要素进行阐述、分析、评价、推理与解释的一系列技能。

思辨能力的重要性应该是不言而喻的。两千多年前的中国古代典籍《礼记·中庸》曰："博学之，审问之，慎思之，明辨之，笃行之。"古希腊哲人苏格拉底说："未经审视的人生不值得一过。"可以说，文明的诞生正是人类自觉运用思辨能力，不断适应并改造自然环境的结果。如果说游牧时代、农业时代以及现代早期，人类思辨能力虽然并不完善，也远未普及，但通过科学技术以及人文知识的不断积累创新，推动人类文明阔步前进，已经显示出不可抑制的巨大能量，那么，进入信息时代、知识经济时代和全球化时代，思辨能力对于人类文明整体可持续发展以及对于每一个体的生存和发展，其重要性将史无前例地彰显。

我们已进入一个加速变化、普遍联系和日益复杂的时代。随着交通技术和信息技术日新月异的发展，不同国家和文化空前紧密地联系在一起。这在促进合作的同时，导致了更多的冲突；人类所掌握的技术力量与日俱增，在不断提高物质生活质量的同时，也极大地破坏了我们赖以生存的自然环境；工业化、城市化和信息化的不断延伸，全方位扩大了人的自由空间，同时却削弱了维系社会秩序和稳定的价值体系与行为准则。这一切变化对人类的思辨能力和应变能力都提出了前所未有的要求。正如本套丛书作者理查德·保罗（Richard Paul）和琳达·埃尔德（Linda Elder）所创办的思辨研究中心的“使命”所指出的，“我们身处其中的这个世界要求我们不断重新学习，习惯性重新思考我们的决定，周期性重新评价我们的工作和生活方式。简言之，我们面临一个全新的世界，在这个新世界，大脑掌控自己并经常进行自我分析的能力将日益决定我们工作的质量、生活的质量乃至我们的生存本身。”

遗憾的是，面临时代巨变对人类思辨能力提出的新挑战，我们的教育和社会都尚未做好充分准备。从小学到大学，在很大程度上我们的教育依然围绕知识的搬运而展开，学校周而复始的考试不断强化学生对标准答案的追求而不是对问题复杂性和探索过程的关注，全社会也尚未形成鼓励独立思辨与开拓创新的氛围。

我们知道，人类大脑并不具备天然遗传的思辨能力。事实上，在自然状态下，人们往往倾向于以自我为中心或随波逐流，容易被偏见左右，固守陈见，急于判断，为利益或情感所左右。因此，思辨能力需要通过后天的学习和训练得以提高，思辨能力培养也因此应该成为教育的不懈使命。

哈佛大学以培养学生“乐于发现和思辨”为根本追求；剑桥大学也把“鼓励怀疑精神”奉为宗旨。美国学者彼得·法乔恩（Peter Facione）一言以蔽之：“教育，不折不扣，就是学会思考。”

和任何其他技能的学习一样，学会思考也是有规律可循的。首先，学习者应该了解思辨的基本特点和理论框架。根据理查德·保罗和琳达·埃尔德的研究，所有的推理都有一个目的，都试图澄清或解决问题，都基于假设，都从某一视角展开，都基于数据、信息和证据，都通过概念和观念进行表达，都通过推理或阐释得出结论并对数据赋予意义，都会产生影响或后果。分析一个推理或论述的质量或有效性，意味着按照思辨的标准进行检验，这个标准由10个维度构成：清晰性、准确性、精确性、相关性、深刻性、宽广性、逻辑性、完整性、重要性、公正性。一个拥有思辨能力的人具备八大品质，包括：诚实、谦虚、相信理性、坚忍不拔、公正、勇气、同理心、独立思考。

其次，学习者应该掌握具体的思辨方法。如：如何阐释和理解文本信息与观点？如何解析文本结构？如何评价论述的有效性？如何把已有理论和方法运用于新的场景？如何收集和鉴别信息和证据？如何论证说理？如何识别逻辑谬误？如何提问？如何对自己的思维进行反思和矫正？等等等等。

最后，思辨能力的提高必须经过系统的训练。思辨能力的发展是一个从低级思维向高级思维发展的过程，必须运用思辨的标准一以贯之地训练思辨的各要素，在各门课程的学习中练习思辨，在实际工作中使用思辨，在日常生活中体验思辨，最终使良好的思维习惯成为第二本能。

“思想者指南丛书”旨在为教师教授思辨方法、学生学习思辨技能和社会大众提高思辨能力提供最为简明和最为实用的操作指南。该套丛书直接从西方最具影响力的思辨能力研究和培训机构（The Foundation for Critical Thinking）原版引进，共21册，包括“基础篇”：《批判性思维术语手册》、《批判性思维概念与方法手册》、《大脑的奥秘》、《批判性思维与创造性思维》、《什么是批判性思维》、《什么是分析性思维》；“大众篇”：《识别逻辑谬误》、《思维的标准》、《如何提问》、《像苏格拉底一样提问》、《什么是伦理推理》、《什么是工科推理》、《什么是科学思维》；“教学篇”：《透视教育时尚》、《思辨能力评价标准》、《思辨阅读与写作测评》、《如何促进主动学习与合作学习》、《如何提升学生的学习能力》、《如何通过思辨学好一门学科》、《如何进行思辨性阅读》、《如何进行思辨性写作》。

由理查德·保罗和琳达·埃尔德两位思辨能力研究领域的全球顶级大师领衔研发的“思想者指南丛书”，享誉北美乃至全球，销售数百万册，被美国中小学、高等学校乃至公司和政府部门普遍用于教学、培训和人才选拔。该套丛书具有如下特点：其一，语言简洁明快，具有一般英文水平的读者都能阅读；其二，内容生动易懂，运用大量的具体例子解释思辨的理论和方法；其三，针对性和操作性极强，教师可以从“教学篇”子系列中获取指导教学改革的思辨教学策略与方法，学生也可从“教学篇”子系列中找到提高不同学科学习能力的思辨技巧；一般社会人士可以通过“大众篇”子系列掌握思辨的通用技巧，提高在社会场景中分析问题和解决问题的能力；各类读者都可以通过“基础篇”子系列掌握思维的基本规律和思辨的基本理论。

总之，思辨能力的高下将决定一个人学业的优劣、事业的成败乃至一个民族的兴衰。在此意义上，我向全国中小学教师、高等学校教师和学生以及社会大众郑重推荐“思想者指南丛书”。相信该套丛书的普及阅读和学习运用，必将有利于促进教育改革，提高人才培养质量，提升大众思辨能力，为创新型国家建设和社会文明进步作出深远的贡献。

孙有中

2016年春于北京外国语大学

Contents

Introduction. 1
1) During Lectures Ask the Class Questions to Arouse Curiosity. 2
2) Use Study Questions. 2
3) Give a Five-Minute Quiz at the Start of Each Class 3
4) Use Charts 3
5) Teach the Principles of Critical Thinking Along with the Subject Matter. . . 3
6) Get Students to Know Each Other 4
7) Put Students' Names on Index Cards and Call on All Students, Not Just Volunteers 4
8) Promote Independent Thinking 5
9) Promote Careful Listening. 5
10) Speak Less So That Students Think More. 5
11) Be a Model. 6
12) Use Socratic Questioning 7
13) Promote Collaboration. 7
14) Try Pyramid Teaching 7
15) Have Students Do Pre-writing. 8
16) Give Written Assignments That Require Independent Thought. 8
17) Have Students Evaluate Each Other's Work 9
18) Use Learning Logs. 9
19) Organize Debates 10
20) Have Students Write Constructive Dialogues. 10
21) Have Students Explain Their Current Assignment and Its Purpose. 11
22) Promote Student Direction. 11
23) Have Students Document Their Progress. 11
24) Break Projects Down. 12
25) Promote Discovery 12
26) Promote Self-Assessment. 13
27) Teach for Usefulness. 13
Summary. 14

Introduction

Although bringing critical thinking into the classroom ultimately requires serious, long-term development, you don't need to sweat and slave to begin to make important changes in your teaching. Many simple, straightforward, yet powerful strategies can be implemented immediately. Below we offer a sampling of such suggestions. They are powerful and useful, because each is a way to get students actively engaged in thinking about what they are trying to learn. Each represents a shift of responsibility for learning from the teacher to the student. These strategies suggest ways to get your students to do the hard work of learning.

Many strategies enable you to take advantage of what students already know and what they are able to figure out for themselves. Many involve students' working together. All too often students get stuck, or don't understand what they are supposed to do. Several students working together can correct each other's misunderstandings and can make much more progress on tasks. When one student gets stuck, another might have just the right idea to move things along. This enables students to become responsible for more of their own learning. Over time, they begin to adopt the strategies they see their peers use successfully and learn to ask themselves critical questions raised by their peers.

Another advantage of the following suggestions is their wide applicability. Most can be fruitfully applied to any subject, any topic. Most can become standard practice—techniques you continually use. For some of these strategies, we provide examples geared to different content they might be used to teach.

At the heart of our approach is a realistic conception of what it takes for someone to learn something. In a sense, much instruction is unrealistic: "If I say it clearly, they should get it. If they give the right answer, they know it and understand it. If I show them what to do, ask them to do it, and they repeat my performance, they have learned the skill and it is theirs whenever they need it. If I tell them why something is true or is important and they nod their heads and repeat it back, they understand the truth or importance of what I have said."

This is not necessarily so. Often students' failure to do well, to apply what they have covered, to remember in the Fall what they learned the previous Spring, results from the above naïve misconceptions about what learning requires. Above all, learning requires thinking — critical thinking. To learn, one must continually ask ,"What does this really mean? How do we know? If it is true, what else would be true?" At the heart of our approach is the conviction that, ultimately, learners must answer these questions for themselves in order to learn, to know, to truly understand. Answers you provide do not entirely sink in unless students' minds are ready to take them in.

The following suggestions, or "teaching tactics," provide ways to begin this process of enabling students to think their way through the material they are expected to learn, to learn how to use what they learn, and use the power of their own minds to "figure things out."

1) During Lectures Ask the Class Questions to Arouse Curiosity.

If students want to know a fact — either because their curiosity has been aroused or because it will be of use in their daily living — they will be motivated to learn it. If the questions asked in class are of a probing nature, they will also lead to a deeper understanding.

2) Use Study Questions.

These can be created for every assignment, lecture, and audio-visual presentation. Students are motivated to quiz themselves, and each other, on these questions because exams are based completely on them. The study questions should require some active thinking, not mere memorization. Some of them should test for the ability to understand, explain, illustrate, and apply the concepts and principles being taught. For instance, in a lesson on human anatomy, before the teacher shows slides of the human heart, study questions are handed out to the class. These questions test specific concepts and general principles. Here are some examples: a) What is a valve? What valves are contained in the heart? What purpose do they serve? b) What is the difference between a vein and an artery? c) What is cholesterol? Why is a high cholesterol level a hazard to one's health? d) Draw a picture of the heart, label each part, and explain how it functions in the total activity of the heart. e) List five functions of the circulatory system and explain how each of these is accomplished. f) Explain how the blood is kept at a constant temperature. g) Define and illustrate by example the principle of "homeostasis." What bodily processes are regulated by this process?

3) Give a Five-Minute Quiz at the Start of Each Class.

These can be a few multiple choice or true/false items derived from study questions. Such quizzes motivate students to go over their classroom notes and keep up with their homework assignments. On their own, students quiz each other on study questions to prepare for exams. Those who are able to understand the material often explain it to the rest in informal groups after class and before tests.

4) Use Charts.

Public speakers have found that the use of charts and simple statements written on tablets placed in front of the audience serve to focus their attention on the question at hand. This method also facilitates assimilation and retention of material. Charts can also be used to tie everything together into a coherent whole — in which all the relationships between the parts are made explicit.

5) Teach the Principles of Critical Thinking Along with the Subject Matter.

Use the material as concrete examples of critical thinking. For instance, when talking about the American Revolution, ask the students to compare the point of view of the Colonists with that of the British Government in a fairminded way. The following study questions could be used to get students to think more deeply and critically about their homework assignment: a) What was the purpose of the Revolution? b) What was the Colonists' concept of freedom? How did it differ from the British concept? c) Why wouldn't the British allow the Colonists to secede from the British Empire? d) What assumptions were made by both sides? e) What evidence was cited by the Colonists which led them to conclude that they were being treated unjustly? Was this evidence accurate? Was it biased? Did they leave out any important facts? f) What were the immediate and long-term consequences of the Declaration of Independence? Exam questions should be based on these study questions to make sure students will think about them, and hopefully quiz each other on them, outside of class. Throughout the lesson, students will learn the elements of reasoning in addition to American history. They will also learn a little about what it is to think fairmindedly and objectively about our nation's history.

6) Get Students to Know Each Other.

On the first day of class, arrange the students in pairs and have members of each pair ask each other questions about where they come from, their interests, hobbies, and opinions—taking notes to facilitate memory. Then each person introduces his or her partner to the whole class. In that way students get acquainted with each other at the outset. This serves to break the ice and facilitates their communication with each other when they are organized into small groups. It is also an effective exercise in attentive listening.

7) Put Students' Names on Index Cards and Call on All Students, Not Just Volunteers.

Have you noticed that when you ask questions in class, the same students always volunteer to give an answer? If you look around the class and pick less active students and ask them a question, they often feel that you are deliberately trying to show up their ignorance, and consequently resent it. So now try putting all the students' names on index cards, shuffle them and ask students questions in a random order. In that way all of the students will listen to your questions, and all will become active in answering them. This simple technique avoids the common problem of four or five students doing most of the talking. It also makes a wider range of student thought available to the class (including the teacher). And it keeps the class more alert.

8) Promote Independent Thinking.

Present students with a problem that requires some independent thinking and has several possible solutions. Have the students write their solutions on a piece of paper. Then divide the class up into groups of three or four, and have them share their answers with their group. Afterwards have each group use the best ideas of each person and have them choose one person to communicate their integrated solution to the class as a whole. In this way all students become active in: 1) figuring out a solution to the problem, 2) communicating their solution to others, 3) obtaining feedback from others, 4) arriving at a more adequate solution to the problem, and 5) occasionally speaking in front of the whole class, thus giving them practice in public speaking.

9) Promote Careful Listening.

Frequently call on students to summarize in their own words what another student has said. This encourages students to actively listen to each other. It helps them realize that they can learn from each other. This serves to lessen their dependence on the teacher for everything. Hearing another student's comments and questions can be quite instructional. Becoming aware of another student's mistakes or misunderstandings and hearing another student correct them also contributes to a clearer understanding. Students who tune out their peers miss these clarifications. Therefore, you should encourage students to consistently and carefully listen to each other in class. One way of doing this is to frequently ask students to repeat what another student just said. That will keep them alert!

Another tactic we advocate fosters careful listening. Arrange students in pairs. Then ask a controversial question. The students then share their opinions with their partners and justify their positions. Their partners listen carefully and then repeat back what was said — but in their own words. The first speakers then point out any misunderstandings of the views they had expressed.

10) Speak Less So That Students Think More.

Try not to lecture more than 20% of total class time. Break off your lecture every ten minutes and have students talk to each other in pairs or threes, where they will retell the key points made, and then apply, assess, or explore the implications of the material.

When you are the one doing most of the talking, you are the one doing most of the thinking. As you explain what you know, you may have to express yourself differently, think of new examples, and make new connections. If you can get your students to do more of the talking, they will be thinking through the material and developing a deeper understanding. As one teacher put it, "Next year my students will be taking my class; I've been taking it for 18 years."

People's minds drift in and out of long speeches, and so they miss much of what is said. Breaking up long lectures gives students a chance to be more active—and also assimilate and think about what they've heard. Smaller bits are easier to mentally digest than large hunks. And, by pooling their perceptions, students can sometimes correct each others' misunderstandings before they become deeply ingrained. Having them report on what they discussed helps the teacher correct their misunderstandings.

11) Be a Model.

Think aloud in front of your students. Let them hear you puzzling your way slowly through problems in the subject. Try to think aloud at the level of the students in the class. If your thinking is too advanced or proceeds too quickly, they will not be able to understand and assimilate it.

Just as you often supplement your verbal instructions by demonstrating to students what you want them to do, it's useful to model for them the kinds of thinking processes you want them to engage in. Modeling careful reading, questioning, or problem-solving conveys much more clearly than verbal instruction alone, the kind of thing you want them to do. It is, therefore, crucial that you model work at their level, not at the level of an expert. This includes making mistakes and reasoning your way out of them. This not only shows students that dead ends and mistakes are unavoidable, but helps teach them how to identify when they may be on one.

12) Use Socratic Questioning.

Regularly question your students Socratically, probing various dimensions of their thinking: What do you mean when you use that word? What point are you trying to make? What evidence do you have to support that statement? Is the evidence from a reliable source? How did you arrive at that conclusion? But how do you account for this? Do you see what that would imply? What would be the undesirable side effects of your proposal? How do you think your opponents view that situation? How might they respond to your argument?

13) Promote Collaboration.

Divide the class frequently into small groups (of twos, threes, fours, etc.) and give the groups specific tasks and specific time limits. Then call on them to report on what part of their task they completed, what problems occurred, and how they tackled those problems. This provides an excellent way for students to accomplish harder tasks and achieve higher quality in their work than they can when working alone. Students can discover much of their course content for themselves by working on well-chosen tasks in small groups before reading or being given explanations by the teacher. Students who frequently have to explain or argue for their own ideas to their peers, and listen to and assess the ideas of their peers, can make significant process in improving the quality of their thought.

14) Try Pyramid Teaching.

Have students discuss a question or problem in pairs to reach consensus. Then have each pair join with another pair to reach consensus. The groups of four then double-up, and so on.

This is an excellent technique for involving every student and developing their confidence in offering their ideas to their peers. It's not hard for them to talk to one other student; and once they have already expressed and clarified their ideas, it's not as hard to talk in groups of four, eight, or sixteen. Not only does each student have to participate, but each student's ideas become part of the final group effort.

It's a way to maximize both the variety and assessment of ideas. Each time the groups are enlarged, an idea is subjected to more scrutiny. Students then realize that the idea needs to be modified. Thus the idea improves in quality with each step.

15) Have Students Do Pre-writing.

Before lecturing or having students read about a topic, have them write rough notes to themselves on that topic for five minutes. They can then use these as the basis for class discussion or small group discussion. This serves several functions. It gets each student actively engaged in thinking about the topic and it activates each student's previous knowledge and experience. As the students think about the material and write down their ideas, they will be able to contribute more effectively in small group and classroom discussions. Finally, since their minds are already grappling with their own and their peers' ideas, students are better able to comprehend and retain new knowledge.

16) Give Written Assignments That Require Independent Thought.

Require regular writing for class. You needn't grade everything they write. You could randomly sample their work, or else have students pick their best work to revise and submit for grading. Having students critique each other's writing can greatly lessen the time you spend reading and commenting on rough drafts. Peer editing provides a way to have students get helpful feedback without over-burdening the teacher. It also develops students' insight into criteria for good writing and ability to notice errors or need for improvement.

It would be hard to overestimate the benefit to quality of thought to be gained from writing — and especially rewriting. Writing forces people to put their thoughts into words, put the words together into complete thoughts, and organize their thoughts into paragraphs that logically flow together. All of this forces students to think more than they otherwise would and develop their thinking further. It also uncovers thought. Students will think of new ideas as they write. And when they read what they have written, they often find reasons for revising them.

Re-writing and revision are essential to developing disciplined thought and expression. When we are forced to look at our work we learn to ask ourselves crucial questions and assess both thought and expression.

17) Have Students Evaluate Each Other's Work.

Give students, or groups of students, the assignment of assessing each other's work. These assignments can take many forms: evaluating and commenting on an individual's work, picking the "best of the group" to be shared with the rest of the class, and suggesting that a student is now ready to turn in an assignment or take a test or quiz. Notes from peer assessments should be turned in.

Peer evaluation has advantages for everyone concerned: it lightens the instructor's load and is useful to both those doing the evaluating and those whose work is evaluated. Students tend to try harder when they know their classmates are going to see their work. They have more internal motivation to put forth their best for "a real audience." They also tend to take comments and suggestions more to heart, rather than attributing criticism to a teacher's arbitrary whim.

But perhaps the greatest advantage is to the students who do the assessing. They gain tremendous insight into standards of good work as they practice applying those standards to work that is not their own. When they justify or explain their comments and suggestions, they are forced to make those standards explicit.

18) Use Learning Logs.

Have students keep two-column notebooks: 1) have them enter the material they get from reading and writing, and 2) have them enter their own thinking reactions to what they are learning. The latter would include: questions, hypotheses, their own reorganization of the material, their own graphs and charts, as well as comments on their thinking processes and progress. These learning logs can be shared in groups, in which students will compare their ideas. Hypotheses and questions can be made the basis of future assignments and special projects; the notebooks can be periodically turned in for your feedback.

19) Organize Debates.

Sometimes have students present debates on controversial issues. For instance, ask how many in the class think that Physical Education should be a required subject for all students in the school. When they raise their hands, choose two or three students who think that it should be required. Ask them to get together and develop their reasoning. Do the same with those who believe that Physical Education should not be required. The groups spend some time in class developing their strategies. They present their debates the next day. Afterwards, students who had no initial opinion on the topic are asked which side had convinced them and explain why.

20) Have Students Write Constructive Dialogues.

Give students a written assignment in which they will imagine dialogues between people with different perspectives on a current issue such as affirmative action or zero-tolerance policies. Dialogues could also be on the different points of view held by opposing sides in an international dispute. There could also be a dialogue between a liberal and a conservative. Students are told that each speaker in the dialogue should be intelligent, rational, and fairminded.

When students are composing a dialogue, they are required to think from different perspectives. Writing dialogues makes it easier for students to enter the perspective held by someone they disagree with—and to do so fairmindedly. It also forces students to have persons with different perspectives address each other: make objections, raise questions, and propose alternatives. Students must then figure out how each will respond. This forces students to further develop their understanding of each perspective, its strengths and weaknesses. It also helps them see why people would hold a particular position and how they would respond to alternative points of view. Students tend to give much stronger arguments for different perspectives when they write dialogues. In order to write an effective dialogue, they have to empathize with those with a point of view they do not accept. Merely describing the point of view of an adversary does not require such empathy.

21) Have Students Explain Their Current Assignment and Its Purpose.

Having students explain the assignment helps clear up misunderstandings before they begin. After they explain the purpose of an assignment in their own words, students will focus more on that purpose. They are more likely to keep their work in keeping with the purpose, rather than running off on tangents.

22) Promote Student Direction.

Have students determine the next step in the study of the current topic. "Given what we now know about this topic, what do you think we should do or focus on next? What information do we need? What do we need to figure out? How can we verify our hypothesis?" Have the class come to a decision about what needs to be done next.

This strategy develops autonomy of thought and intellectual responsibility. It puts some of the burden on students to recognize what they need to address. Independent thinkers need to develop the habit of taking stock of where they are, what they know, and what they need to know. Putting this decision up to the class gives students some sense of control over what they will be doing. It thus creates greater involvement on the part of students and greater commitment — hence greater motivation.

23) Have Students Document Their Progress.

Tell students to write what they think about a topic before they begin study. Then after the lesson, have them write down their current thinking about the topic and compare it with their initial thoughts. One advantage of this tactic is that it gets students thinking about a topic before exposure to what the teacher and text have to say. Its greatest strength, however, is that it vividly demonstrates to students the progress they have made. It's all there on paper for them to see how their thinking has changed. You can even make this a part of your grading — giving some credit on the basis of how much progress each student has made.

24) Break Projects Down.

Assign a series of small writing assignments, each on a sub-topic of a larger topic. The final assignment, then, can be to re-write the sections as one longer work. Later, have students design similar series of assignments for themselves when they get stuck on projects. Students who are stymied by large tasks often fail to break them down into more approachable tasks. Giving students small, relatively easy assignments enables them to complete each one as a unit — much less daunting than one large paper. By combining the small writings into one larger piece, students not only have to rethink what they have done, but they have been enabled to complete a large, more sophisticated piece of writing. They develop confidence in their ability to do longer projects.

25) Promote Discovery.

Design activities in which students discover insights, principles, and techniques for themselves before presenting material through lecture or reading. For instance, one typing teacher, rather than giving students the complicated formula for centering a table on a page, gave them the task of figuring out how to type a centered table. Having the class brainstorm in response to a problem facilitates such discoveries. These activities are usually best done in small groups, rather than individually. It is also instructive to have students discuss the problems they encountered and how they overcame them.

Whatever students discover for themselves will be more deeply understood. They will not only learn that it is so, but will understand why it is so. Students gain crucial practice in figuring things out and solving problems for themselves, rather than having to be told what to do and how. Furthermore, the more experiences they have of discovering important knowledge for themselves, the more confidence they will have in their own thinking abilities.

When students become involved with an independent project, they sometimes become highly motivated and do more independent thinking. Such projects should be encouraged. Periodic supervision and words of appreciation help sustain motivation.

26) Promote Self-Assessment.

Spell out explicitly the intellectual standards you will be using in your grading. Teach the students how to assess their own work, using those standards. You might first have students formulate what they consider to be the criteria by which their work should be judged. The class can then discuss the appropriateness of each proposed criterion. Another way to teach students self-assessment is to give them copies of old student papers (an A paper, a C, and a D names removed of course), and have them assign a letter grade to each. Then, have students work in small groups to come to consensus on the grades and the criteria. Whole class discussion can share the results of this and give you the opportunity to raise any points students missed.

The criteria by which you judge student work is more obvious to you than to your students. Being able to enumerate the criteria is not at all the same as actually being able to use them. To recognize when these criteria are met and when they are not, and be able to re-work something to bring it closer to high standards is something that requires considerable practice. Students don't gain these abilities by reciting abstract principles. Teaching students how to assess their own work is one of the most important things you can do to get them to improve the quality of their work.

27) Teach for Usefulness.

Teach concepts, as far as possible, in the context of their use as functional tools for the solution of real problems and the analysis of significant issues. We learn what we value knowing. When students are simply told that what they learn is valuable, but don't actually experience that value and power, they tend to disbelieve, or not truly believe, that there is any point to what they learn.

We should continually demonstrate the value of what we are teaching. No amount of abstract argument will engender the deep, sincere conviction that knowledge is valuable. Such a conviction requires the experience of actually using it. If students begin with an interesting question or problem, and find they can make much more progress on it when they have the insights and skills which a lesson provides, they will gain a greater appreciation of the material in that lesson.

By "taking in" material without applying it to significant issues, students do not learn how to apply what they learn. The best way to solve the problem of transfer is to not create it in the first place. Transfer is impeded when teachers divorce learning from application or postpone fruitful application indefinitely.

Summary

These tactics, and others like them, are useful in generating greater student involvement in the subject matter. They promote active listening and get more individuals to participate in classroom discussions. Students also learn how to summarize the views of others. When students express and justify their own opinions and yet learn to respond empathetically to the ideas of others, they are beginning to use some of the most important abilities required in critical thinking.

Getting students actively thinking about what they are learning in itself is not enough. We don't merely want students to think, but to think well. The tactics we covered do something in this direction. Teachers who use these tactics tend to find distinct, even surprising, improvement in the quality of students' thinking. Still, students best develop critical thinking abilities when they are explicitly taught how to think about their thinking.

In doing this, we need to focus on the analysis and evaluation of reasoning. This involves breaking thinking into its component parts and scrutinizing each part: purpose, question at issue, concepts, assumptions, evidence, conclusions, and implications. Critical thinking activities are essential for analysis and evaluation. In this miniature guide we have not focused on the various component critical thinking skills, traits, and standards.

Finally, we need to introduce critical thinking abilities in a holistic fashion, combining all the separate skills to form a deeper understanding of a subject matter and discover relationships between all its parts. The logic of a discipline needs to be clarified. Insights gained while studying one issue should be transferred to gain an understanding of other issues. Interdisciplinary approaches are used to examine a problem from different perspectives. We focus on these other important goals in other miniature guides. For example, consult *The Guide to Critical Thinking* and *How to Study and Learn* in this set.